Crows Nest

A Collection of Poetry

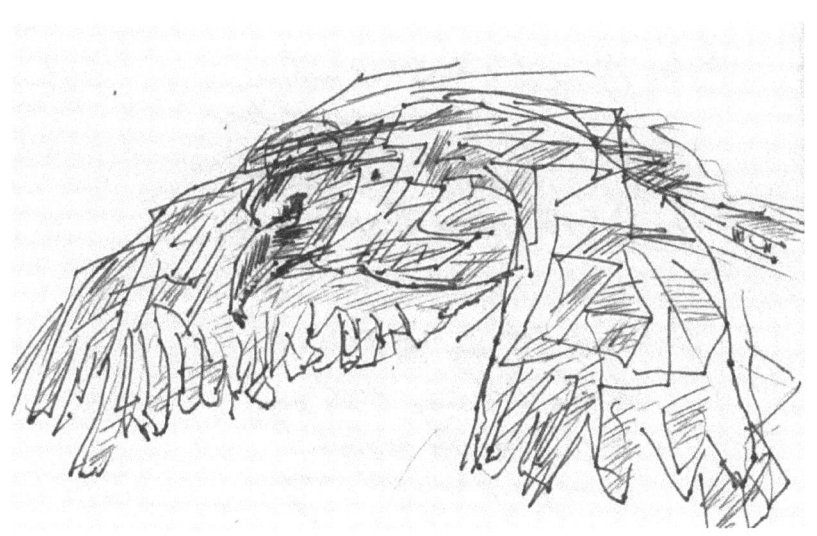

Marc Savett

NFB
<<<>>>
Buffalo, NY

Copyright © 2015 Marc Savett

Printed in the United States of America

Savett, Marc

Crows Nest/ Savett- 1st Edition

ISBN: 978-0692409497

1. Crows Nest – Poetry– Verse.
No Frills.
Title

No part of this book may be reproduced or transmitted in any form by any means, electronic or mechanical, including photocopying, recording, or by any information storage and retrieval system without permission in writing by the author.

No Frills Buffalo/Amelia Press
119 Dorchester Buffalo, New York 14213
For more information visit
Nofrillsbuffalo.com

For Bukowski who gave me the courage to write a poetry book

Contents

Kafka's Eyes	7
Ahab's Fate	8
Mariachi Guitar	9
Sanctuary	10
Lion's Pride	11
Mexican Cat	12
The Sentence and the Period	13
Honey Moon	14
Facsimiles of Cleopatra	15
Amiguismo- Exchanging Favors	17
Surf Green Mercury	18
Stone House	19
Tripods Revenge	20
Don's Voice	21
Will and His Mother	22
Sapphire Eyes	23
Unshackling	24
Robert Johnson Ode	25
Evil Genies	26
Edge of the World	27
Summer Reminisce	28
Amish Horse	29
Romantic Rendevouz	31
Vesuvius	33
Bullets and Butterflies	34
Two Marionettes	35
Suspense	36
Hitting Needles	37
Bombers	38
Hard Fall	39
Eagle Egg Hatching	40
Devil's Hum	41
Egypt's Gift	42
Sidewalk Pimp	44
A Brother's Tyranny	45
Blood Painting	46
Cousin Larry	47

Gunslinger	48
Pirates on Mead	49
Stewardship	50
Button Box	51
White Fox	52
Marta's Dream	53
Rodents and Lice	54
High Sierra	55
King Kong 1933	56
Killer	58
Six Corpses	59
Snakes on Matted Grass	60
Coffee Shop Earshot	61
Cloud Forest Creature	62
Russian Bar	63
Bad Fish	64
American Bandstand	65
Golden Frogs	66
Antiquity	67
Playground Mandala 1976	68
Billie	69
Value of Life	71
Children in White Robes	72
Twisted Virtue	74
The Invisibility of Outrage	75
Poetry Reading	76
Virtual Virus Riot	77
Nutritive Absence	78
Irreverent Chorus	79
Old Shoe	80
Monsters	81
Refugees	82
Nightmares and Ghosts	83

KAFKA'S EYES

On Charles Bridge I looked into Kafka's eyes
He turned away as if amidst some incendiary vision
Of the future his writings burning

Kafka conjured twisted tomorrows
His perspective dehumanization evil scientists,
And mad machines of death
He could touch the space
Between imagination and metal monsters

Trains and poison gas were on the horizon
The holocaust a trembling premonition

Loved ones swallowed by the camps
His sense of humor preserved buoyancy
As he was being devoured by TB microbes in
The box of his apartment

Smetana's Moldau, the symphonic poem
Emanates from the Prague National Theatre
Driving the Czechs to dance madly in the streets
As if beetles were crawling up their nostrils
Prior to diving into the icy river.

Somewhere dark in the world
Night is falling
The masses are skittering
Toward burrows where they enjoy only a restless sleep.

AHAB'S FATE

There were cages that held hostage Birds of Paradise
Promising salvation. By chains ropes pulleys and harpoons
The old man was being dragged deeper into the blue sea.
He imagined himself the whale his tail slapping the waves
Free and unrestrained by human intervention. His visions
Were empowering while tethered to a hospital bed with twenty five
Tubes running from veins arteries stomach bladder and heart.
Nurses cleaned him top to bottom. There was constant beeping
Lights flashing alarms interns residents attendings stopping
In for examination. He was poked pried and picked over. Cardiologists spent
A few minutes delivering Texas smiles prior to Leaving his room.
He was the great whale slowly being dragged down
Below the surface. There was too much weight on his back to
Stay buoyant smashed with repeating triads of breakers. Till
The end he fought back with his provincial vocabularies. Revenging
Evil with spikes and nails. He infused me with hard metal folded
Over my heart. He was a gray man looking at me down on my knees.
I sat beside the whale circumvented in tubes listening to a cacophony
Of alarms beeps buzzers and bells. After six weeks in cardiac care
He dove deep looking for a battle with a worthy squid. For years
We were impaled on the body of that great beast. Just as much
Energy was required to disengage from his domination. We threw
His ashes high where there are no more moments of life.

MARIACHI GUITAR

He practiced guitar
Sequestered in his flat for a week
He mastered ten basic chords
Hopped a train one sunny day
Jalisco to Tijuana
Catching a series of rides
To San Francisco

He played his Mariachi Guitar
On the buses in the Mission District
Struck with his fingers
The lyrics were emeralds and diamonds
Strung on a platinum chain
Dancing around his neck
His chords strummed rhythms
Into tangos and rumbas
That woke coffee-eyed commuters

The bus moved in and out of arpeggios
Winding around passengers' ears
Swaying their heads to the rhythm
Vibrating from the nylon strings

They thanked him with a smile
A few tossed coins into his hat
As he stepped off the bus
With a large Mariachi Guitar
On his back

SANCTUARY

Ten years they prepared for the journey
Wearing feathers of the oriole and cardinal
Through his hair to remind him of his beginnings
With raw voice and guns in his eyes
He believed in a spoon for a spoon of justice
Classmates were glued in study like a minor religion
As he purchased hard voyage
Those priests pattered through his mind
Like squirrels in an attic
He gilded his cage with gold fabric
From the gulf of Siam which he exchanged
For ivory and emeralds in Shanghai
Ten times he faced death
Then rose from his ashes
The loadstone was his homestead
Electric in his mind
With cellars stacked with casks
Of honeyed single malt
He lay inebriated inside its fragrant memories
As he was chased by pirates and starved in prison
Which stripped away his virtues
As he was bitten by beasts
Then incapacitated by typhus
Death grinned from above and below
While riches filled the cargo hatch
Broken from captivity images materialized
Of beginnings and endings
There were strange flute calls
Friends danced finding sanctuary
in his grit and courage

LION'S PRIDE

When the lion is driven from his pride
He remembers all rivals who have humiliated
The throne rampages are merely self-deception
The beast imagines his alpha role
Still his as he wanders the land in isolation
There is risk without family with death following close
In pursuit of his failing substance

His roar is only a whisper
That bargains for a few weeks
Beaten he recalls each battle
With hardened rivals
Written on his coat in scar tissue
Violent hallucinations open the king
To possession by demons that flatter
Though cannot save him from his fall

MEXICAN CAT

Colima Mexico early morning
An ocelot sniffs the salty air
Leaping across a costal dirt road
The cat's killed by the family car

On return to the city
They learn of their
Aunt's sudden death
From a heart attack
The sleek cat decays on the roadside
The living are tainted by nausea

The ocelot
Running biting and scratching
In the family's brain
The wild creature sinking teeth
Into quicksand

THE SENTENCE AND THE PERIOD

The sentence was like a battering ram
He liked to charge straight away
As if there was nothing before him
This led to no shortage of complications
Often he would bust right through the period
Obliterating the beginning of the next sentence
Absolutely splintering it into oblivion
The period tried to coach the sentence to slow down
And actually stop before proceeding toward
The yellow and red traffic light up ahead
That would let all meaning pass in time

The impulsive sentence frequently
Argued with the period for days
He just couldn't accept that such a small dot
Could exert such control over him

Wasn't he the agent of meaning?
The stuff that great novels are born from?
The period exclaimed that he was only trying to instill order
For there to be meaning
There must be regulation
Or all significance could be distorted

After repeated destruction of its structure
The sentence began to respect the period
They finally both signed a truce
That led to an explosive growth in science and literature

Summary:
Refusing to negotiate hatches chaos

HONEY MOON

The honeymoon was a volcano running into the surf
It gobbled him up under a full moon
He lay still paralyzed by the brash decision
To take on the huge crashing breakers
As if he was fighting for the heavy weight title
That he lost that night in the twilight

Perhaps he should have worn his glasses
As the myopia blurred the size of the thunderous waves
That spread like a mountain range before him
Washing him to the shore his neck broken

Red lights flashed against the stony cliffs
Ambulances screamed unholy howls
Along the sandy beach
While hot hips swayed back and forth
To Hawaiian slide guitar on the patio

His wife frozen with panic
Helpless to connect the nerves with the muscles
That ignite the magic harmony of movement
Of a man never to walk against the sunrise
Or stand in front of a sun burning him
In the flames of indigo gold

On the jet plane he lay supine
Trying to find sweet passage
Sucked into the endless night sky
A reading light shone down on him
Like a yellow monstrous Cyclops

FACSIMILES OF CLEOPATRA

Buddies in the university were now trafficking
Pot and coke to college virgins that had no concept
Of hard time in jail cells with a sink and toilet
The big city students were on a first name basis
With dealers who wholesaled good stuff cheap
Talking revolution poetry jams with Marxists
Studying on amphetamines soaring on scenes
Of underground movie festival car crashes
Rambling through the fun house
Kicking hopelessness and ennui further down the road
Pulling all nighters on acid hallucinating white rabbits
Devouring the men's dormitory
Under the autumn dipper

Hipsters shooting heroin into veins dying in the halls
As midnight women accept invitations to sleep
With lonely hearts without names
Chess game chic in wonderland as rock and rollers on FM
Entertained like a late night Rock Festival
Philosophy students bathed in existentialism
Which some thought was study of alien races;
Poets and bluesmen became fixtures bending strings and minds
Roommates passed out pot laced with amphetamines
That pulled them centrifugally down the rabbit hole

Thought became disjointed writing withered on the vine.
Social intercourse swallowed academia
Cleopatras wandered the halls as narcos were busting
Naïve potheads lost through the doors of perception
Detectives hunting mommies' boys were miles beyond
Small timers looking for a kick
The busted were bound to their parole officer
Who gave the convicted a lesson in photo journalism
They spent an hour viewing gangsters
With cocks neatly tucked in their mouths
The goddesses that spread the LSD nonsense

Lowballed the risk to Apollos
Never appraising them to the dangers on the mountains
That would place a barbell on a young man's back
That could never be removed.

AMIGUISMO- EXCHANGING FAVORS

The final examination was a prelude before the prize
While the key was creation of harmony wrapped in philanthropy
Amiguismo or cronyism was in the spine of Mexico
Shrewdness was intelligence tailored to shifting outcomes
The owl held in high esteem epitomized the character of wisdom

A clever plan could fly one home comfortably at semester's end
A tribute was undertaken for the esteemed professors
Our spokesman requested permission to purchase
Four sets of radial tires gifted to the teachers
For the fine education imparted to our class
Wrapped in red ribbons the offering put a broad smile
On our teachers' faces

Most were in concert with gifting
While others considered it unethical
Without fanfare the players passed the exams
Boarding planes bound for the US
Many choosing not to participate in the tribute
Failed finals spending three weeks longer in Guadalajara
Studying a second final exam while walking the campus like zombies
In the end giving is SALUD

SURF GREEN MERCURY

She was a surf green shag top Mercury
She could do one hundred miles per hour chased by the cops
Though suffered a huge appetite of twelve miles per gallon
The '53 had been a looker
She sits in the middle of a cow field
Her engine clogged with the gunk of a lifetime
Neighboring Junkers are carted away to Elysian Fields
Pounded into polygons of scrap metal

No sense of straightening out a crinkle in the hood
Or bringing to life a rusty carburetor
There was no sparkle in the old girls eyes
The surf green in her day was a beauty
Like a slinky Loretta Young brunette
Wearing apple orchid lipstick
She was self-conscious as an octogenarian exposed
Laying alone in her cold plot
Frozen up inside the shag top covered with snow
Cows singing all around her

STONE HOUSE

Slate shingles fell off the roof
Fish in the figure eight concrete
Pond stopped swimming breast
Stroke. The old mansion attracted
Realtors looking for a quick sale
The inhabitants neither cared of
Consequence or revenge

Her weight was crushing on their backs
She was sentimental frosting up around
Her windows when the movers arrived
They packed it up leaving an empty shell
The fear of nothingness expired as her
Candle burnt down

The event reverberated
Earthquakes of emotion that took years
Of forgetting before remembering
After the abandonment she was raped
By grave robbers looking for an easy
Heist. There were no longer cars in her
Driveway. It was too late for regrets
Everyone was going pell-mell their own
Way as she was lost behind a veil

TRIPODS REVENGE

The tripods of elm boughs
Were placed strategically
Like a soldier might lay a land mine

For children it was exquisite music
As the cars crashed into the branches
With a loud sonic boom

We celebrated the process
Proud of our success
Stopping the speeders
As the tripods exploded like supernova

Acting out our actions
Of deconstructionist art and anarchy
We rejoiced in pyrrhic victories
Over the ostentatious muscle cars

Beautiful monstrosities
They were speed demons
With no reverence for naïve children

That might splinter
Like our wooden tripods
From an unsuspected frontal blow

DON'S VOICE

Jackknifing over furniture and missed the call
Just a canned message for voter registration
Sounded like the yoga teacher
Trees shaking leaves, clouds blowing
Through the daily mantra
Forty years since residence in Mexico
The future closer than my beginnings
Obsessions betray the scaffolding of my mind
Identity is mystery
Apparitions sweep the byways

The mysteries of life are thick with question
Juan called from New Jersey with the message
"God bless you I am dead"
Existential insanity since I have
Never communicated interacted with
Or known this individual
There is a voice mail on my phone
Frightening when I least expect him
It begins "if you are M. Zavotsky
This is Don Sartor. Please return my call
If this is the right number. If this is the wrong number
I apologize and will call later.

This is a pina colada of dread
From a dear friend
Dead two years
Stuck in the bytes of my cell phone
My dilemma is inspired desperation
If this message disappears
I erase Don's voice forever
An option too excruciating
To fathom

WILL AND HIS MOTHER

There was a downtown campus in Guadalajara
Where we took clinical course work
It was built as an atrium four floors with a fountain in the center
An open courtyard
There was the smell of sitting water and gardenias
Will frequently gave us a ride uptown
Toward Minerva Circle where we would catch buses home.

I lived west, Dan north of Minerva.
Will had an old VW bug, kind of beat up
He was tall lanky his speech formal and stilted
He exuded an imploding pressure that seemed to pull him inward
There was a morose shyness about him
We in our white lab coats dress shirts pants and ties
Would walk to the VW just small talk generally
About class

Then we drove uptown past restaurants stores and theaters
Tropical trees flourished on the center strip with flowers bordering the
Sidewalk. It was Christmas time a two-week vacation from school
Some students drove or flew home others stayed in Guadalajara
Will was going to fly up to Colorado to see his family
Dan went back to St. Louis I stayed in Guadalajara
Word was after vacation that Will didn't return
He had killed his mother with a knife leaving her in a pool of blood.
We thought an act like this was not beyond Will
Who seemed like he could blow like an improvised explosive device

SAPPHIRE EYES

Cat women live in squalor
They're on a mission to save the world
Often sick with delusions
Their robe is a patron saint
They collect creatures
Hunting them then placing them in
The dollhouse
An artificial environment without bars
Where cats robbed from the street
Or shelter run wild
The alpha cat is a woman Jesus
Dying on a cross to save her pets
Covered with parasites
Neglected by the caretaker
Her house rotting from within
Saturated with feces and urine
That permeates until it destroys livability
A hundred felines imprisoned
Hissing diseased and starving
The cat woman looks calmly over
Her multitude
Breathing stinking air
Content that her work has been delivered
Her sapphire eyes look back at her
As she stares in the mirror

UNSHACKLING

She weeps clutched in her golden cage
Bearing scars of solitude
Living in reminisce
Tears melting present woes
To free the sweet song
Like intoxicating perfume
Into the future
….singing out into the dark night

Imprisoned in her silent space
The finch begins to sing
To optimism and hope
As a chirping Siamese cat
Begins to dance in step
To songs of freedom
….calling out into the dark night

Opening the wire door
To a future that suits the sweet bird
Feathering her soft bed
To consummate frozen dreams
….singing out into the dark night

Though hesitancy and wing beats
Cry to be unchained
The past opened many highways
….calling out into the dark night

Now is the time for flight
While she can envision the passageway
Through the clouds
Old scars fall away
….singing out into the dark night

ROBERT JOHNSON ODE

A young itinerate black musician plays for a few bucks
Hitching a car or hopping a freight
The soles of his feet aching from walking the countryside
His fingers like spidery appendages
Crawl the guitar frets from juke joint to juke joint
Jealousy flutters around the room
No one plays like this
Unless the devil is knocking around his bones
His eyes look out like red coals
While dogs bark, a wild cat in the bush screams
He is singing in an eerie falsetto
Sending chills up everyone's spine

His whiskey is poisoned by a venomous barmaid
Her boyfriend snaps a whip over her head
Patrons are gyrating arms and legs flying
A hunter's moon shoots through the clouds
Dancers' silhouettes spin a kaleidoscope on the walls
The dust is hungry sucking fluid from his pores
The country blues are a dull ache
As the boy barks on the floor
Though there is violent innuendo
The cops can't stick a charge
The tavern door swings open as he jumps a lightning bolt
The devil shares his carriage moaning and howling
Taking him far above thorny misery

EVIL GENIES

They are evil genies of electronics
Masters that envision tremolo fuzz reverb
And delay madness that sits in transistors
And capacitors in small iron enclosures called pedals
That salivate to be touched and turned on
Hot between a guitar and amplifier that blows
The sound out big putting you in the middle of the voice

Of the pedal chain throbbing rubbing kissing
Your ears with quakes demonic,
Sweet as honey cutting and slashing scales
In synchrony of several nasty iron pedals
Chorusing distorting and overdriving
With perverse sustain that begs one to caress a guitar
Mad scientists all vying for a spot on your pedal board

They plead on their knees for an audition
Of their auditory ecstasy that will light up eyes with fireworks
I warn the uninitiated of the menacing allure of these magic boxes
Deceptive syrupy tone that will hook your ears
As you crash on the shoals as the sounds rhythmically
Continue to wash through the brain
Pulling one through black holes into the starry dynamo

EDGE OF THE WORLD

Joni's falling off the edge of the world
Dreamers, doubters, believers
Tripping down wormholes,
Teetering on the steely precipice,
Falling off toward parallel universes.

We don't have the steam to save this place.
Pulling for a little magic, a hero, a song to sing
Some contentment through the darkness.
Can't control Mozart's Requiem
It's melody flowing from my ears through the hip hop nights
The slow march off the ledge

Anger consolidated with revenge turned upside down
Taking the entire planet hostage to the whims of maniacs.
Last opportunity for azure valleys and fertile pastures.
Cesspools of lakes the Great Oceans
Chemical dumps, nuclear wastes,
Desperate individuals working,
20% unemployment in the twilight of life

Elephants, Rhinos, Rich, Poor, the disenfranchised
Overwhelming Noah's Ark
Flowing toward the chute,
Shot down to the edge of the world
Law tablets will be broken, extinctions subtract the present.
Decaying bodies will wake us from the nightmares and kiss us Goodnight.
Cities digested by microbe invasions, populations run from invisible
Enemies
Frightened to the edge of the world.

SUMMER REMINISCE

She called late summer
Playing forgotten chords
I remembered her wicked sarcasm
With neatly brushed wit
Slamming the romantic brakes
As we lay in grasses
Along the steep gorge
Above the gurgling stream
Flowing from Ithaca to Cayuga Lake

There was tentative desperation
In her voice
Holding the passion
Of sweet breath
Against the warmth of teen bodies
Quickly it was over
Passing opportunity
With scant explanation
As I hung the phone on its cradle

She flowed backwards
Toward interstellar vacuum
Hands still tangled in heart's fire
Don Quixote bowing before her
Offering his steed to carry her home
Shakespeare reading a sonnet
To melt her will
Dickinson lost in rhyme of love beauty
And mystery
Heart beats pulse through clouds
Lost in reminisce

AMISH HORSE

The Amish horse reached
His rite of passage
Blushing as his
Bearded owner looked on
In admiration of youth
The animal easily pulling
The inky black carriage
Transporting his master
Adorned in a black suit
To the sawmill
Summer heat glazed
The gelding's eyes
His snout covered in spittle
Climbing and descending
Steep hills
He in time despised his master
Overzealous with the whip
Full of electricity popping off
His adolescent rump
The buggy stood behind
Welding connection
By shaft and leathers
A fiery breath singed his loin
He could hear his master's taunts
Through the automobile horns
Exhaust and squealing tires
Pulling the imponderable weight

Morning unto night
With the passing years
The carriage's weight
Became a mountain of lead
Slowly swallowing the horse
Into a thick fog
Muscles twitched as he
Stood alone

Sweat pouring from
His chestnut coat
The carriage's blackness
Sucked at him like a giant insect
There was no separation
From the buggy
Death flattered and
Then consumed

The Adonis of youth
The Amish horse

ROMANTIC RENDEVOUZ

I recall a man ruffled, a film on his face
Talking to himself in an inner tongue
Difficult to decipher as he would walk past me
Entering the cavernous city library
I would look up from the sturdy oak table
He would be standing in front of a painting
With a sweet smile
The only smile in his dusky day

He stared intently at the beautiful peasant girl
With her radiant features of youth
In her black velvet dress with white bodice
Above her striped vermilion and gray apron
Standing resolutely at her wooden cutting table
Peeling one potato at a time that she chooses
From a burgundy terracotta bowl

Slices of potato skin scatter on the cutting board
Some appear to be held in suspension
Falling upon her apron
Her house is thick stained oak slats
The walls hold shelves with ceramic tea cups
Upside down on saucers
A collection of long-stemmed green translucent wine bottles
Are huddled in one corner of the kitchen

The man begins his conversation with her
His speech strange and unintelligible
He hears her soothing voice which sounds like his own
As he places himself inside the frame
Into a three dimensional comfort
That is lost to him when the library is closed
Daily he makes his pilgrimage from his walk-up to join his love

She never looks him in the eye
Though the radiant beauty of her continence and voice

Bring him sustenance
As he joins her drinking thick red wine,
Eating her delicious potato pie
Kissing her cheek
Explaining silently to her that he must get back
To his work in the field
One last glance, he scans the frame,
Trying to catch her eye as he shuffles away
Over the marble floor, echoing his steps
Off the high ceilings as he walks toward the door

VESUVIUS

We are no longer young men saturated in testosterone
But frozen routines squeezing a last dime from the account
We march toward steep cliffs prior to the leap into the void
Where fish wait with open mouths

Tyranny of memory shackles the present
Some are caught in nightmares of their childhood
Scraping plates for a meal
We are slaves to security after years of travail
Rhetoric rarely turns adverse circumstance

The frail tremble in front of uncertainty
Maggots crawl inside Death
Questioning his taste in décor
Vesuvius smokes in the distance
The heart pumps though blood lies static

An elder asks how deep is the pond
Feet no longer touch bottom
Winds blow through the poppies and daffodils
There is still pleasure conquering small hills

A wise man visualizes complexity
Through gradations of danger
As we swim about the surface

BULLETS AND BUTTERFLIES

Day dreaming supine on a boulder
Looking into the grand canyon of Guadalajara
Raptors dive sharply from jagged cliffs
An obscure form hovers in the distance
Shimmering above the rim reflecting bits of sunlight
Creeping slow time toward my near rim position

A mile below the river meanders
As if two children pulse a jump-rope
In lazy sine waves
Large morpho butterflies flash beauty
Off blue iridescent wings

The sun falls behind the canyon's south face
Shrouded terror becomes clearer
The shape changer pushes outward
In myriad directions
Swarming toward three large boulders

The bees like pellets strike the granite
Hornets in a ball roll over my position
I hug the boulder tight motionless
Discouraging the insects from stinging
As blood throbs through my body

The sonorous droning of wild bees
Rolls over the canyon's rim
Until they disappear far above
Women laundering by the river

TWO MARIONETTES

Two wooden marionettes dance on a stage
Leaping high into an inland sky
They are guided by a puppeteer
Who stands behind the screen
Pulling strings high and low
They smoke as they laugh
Sitting rigidly at a table

They move their heads as if they had just heard
The most outrageous story or joke
They slowly disappear
Absorbed as if they never existed
Then where there were two
There are six million marionettes
Pinpoints on the platform
They move in a concentric circle
Around a large stone column

They walk slowly though they seem to
Know their fate
There is a dirge playing in the background
The marionettes appear then disappear
Leaping off the stage
Then a flicker, a flame
And six million are swallowed into the tissues
Before most can gather their hats
Coats infants and memories

SUSPENSE

She is suspense. A wine glass falling toward another impasse;
Her eyes are dark heavy stones that sit on my beating heart.
Her smile pulls me forward through starry nebulae.
Her laugh brings rain that sweetens the cane with
Lightness of lips and buoyancy of a kiss; an enigma,
She's a flame that balances on a golden candle stick.

HITTING NEEDLES

Mike Bloomfield and Jimi Hendrix guitar icons
Fell through a decade memories an incessant clicking
Like a sick metronome
Wraiths resting their heads on their shoulders
All sweet syrup sucked from their tree
Gig after gig of curtain calls and blinding light
Artists deceived by devious handlers
The next tour-stop a heroin acid explosion
A hypnotic road of helplessness
With no certain escape
Hope tangled in a spider's orb
Legends congeal in the paste of a pair of jokers
Hitting needles walking into darkness barefoot
Beasts talking in foreign tongues
As guitar strings writhe like snakes
The icons try to hide from the smell of years
Laying down another track
They're programmed to fall into fire
Walking on coals
Gold in their teeth and diamonds
In the eye sockets
Dogs growl from hades
Escape was never part of the mythos

BOMBERS

A pressure cooker of war with poverty
Bedfellows that leak desperation through sad hearts
Schools that open children's minds to terror
Strap on explosives hidden in ancient doctrines
Blowing themselves to smithereens
Visions of virgins and flashes of god
Tasting the beginning and end of time
Rings of death subjugate the powerful
Ships crash on shoals
Children float in lifeboats
Bombers scheme to shoot the king's army like dogs
Messengers are sent to poison the kingdom
Subjects lop off the head of order
Poverty breeds starving monstrosities
Governments are thrown on their back
Anarchists set fire to libraries

The western world scowls sitting on dynamite
Senators talk in code to buy time
Violins scream throwing wind toward the fire
Vestal virgins dance on the oasis
Mujahedeen seek the afterlife
In the shifting sands of the desert dunes

HARD FALL

He didn't notice the danger
Playing with the
Small white scorpion

We multitask
A Chinese circus
Spinning ten plates
In the air on stakes
Simultaneously

We use the MP3 and the cell
Driving a two lane at 70mph
By the time you look up
From tuning the HD radio
You are curled inside
The twists of steel

The distractions
Are excruciatingly
Intoxicating
The sirens singing
Lower your eyelids
To a soft sleep
The sun's white glare
Blinding sight

They never open a book
All semester
Plunging into the pit,
Sounding as if they hit hard

EAGLE EGG HATCHING

A joker laughs at a straight flush
Of grifters and question marks that walk past
Dreamers wait for answers to be carved
Into the furrows of their forehead
It is spring when the gypsies percolate
Up through the mesh of soil
Unraveling their intrigues
The elder wears a black tuxedo
Tilting his lover entangled in scarlet tango
They mount steeds cantering along a stone wall
Protected by glass shards
Reflecting sunlight on a knife's edge

Eyes stare heavy through smoke and desire
Scorpions lurk in the abyss
Horses turn to the mountains
Enshrouded in dust devils
They ride hard like two characters
Inside the boundaries of a canvass
Applying pigments to their future
Rifles echo from the canyon below
Sand falls through the spaces between fingers
As they imbibe mescal
Salty like the ocean that opens the heart
An eagle egg hatching

DEVIL'S HUM

We drove narrow roads through rain forest to San Blas, north of Acapulco.
San Blas, a Janus, two faces: One forward in light; one Backward in darkness
during the day there is the Pacific
Slow six foot triads crushing the beach in blue light
The night is an avenging angel

That day the palms rustled in the wind
Green-gray iguanas skittered about the beach
Don and I sat at a wooden table on the beach playing chess, drinking Dos
Equis. We were rapidly losing day
Two riders bareback on stallions were galloping the beach
Suddenly an ocean wind shook the cabana

Shuey, a Mexican fisherman, was smiling toothless over my shoulder
The focus on chess consumed us as if we were devoured by a fire
I looked at Don whose eyes teared up; I wanted to continue the game
Though night was approaching
Shuey exclaimed "Vamos"

All around was an opaque cloud
Of thousands of blood sucking
Mosquitoes and sand fleas
The riders turned their steeds galloping toward Hotel Colon
Don and I sprinted in the horses' wake
Into the waxing drone

EGYPT'S GIFT

I took a quick right
There were red lights flashing
I felt the torture begin
The bus driver peered out the open door
While we waited
Suddenly the front door
Of the house opened

The first daughter emerged
Like the Egyptian priestess Isis
Eyes straight ahead, back straight
Gait deliberate as if her internal clock
Started to fall behind real time
I tapped my fingers on the steering wheel
Ruminating bad thoughts

By some miracle
The second daughter
Stepped through the threshold into her day
Holding books in her arms
As if an offering
As she moved carefully to dream time
As if neither my car or the bus existed

Several minutes elapsed
When incredibly
The third daughter emerged
Making her way to the school bus
I sat in my car quite exercised
As she stepped slowly to
A languorous tone
Ascending the stairs of the bus
Walking down the isle
Taking her seat

Soon after they journeyed to school

On the yellowish morning rays
Of the sun god Ra

SIDEWALK PIMP

New York City on winks of sleep
Faces mirrored in the greyhound bus windows
Nodding off under the Hudson River
Deep in the Lincoln Tunnel

The sidewalk pimp my guide promised angels
Just down the hall waiting for me in their boudoir
Wearing his cabbie hat he seemed benign
Offering Puerto-Rican, Chinese and Black women
A college boy wrapped in reverie
Diving into cloudy waters with dangerous fish

Anticipating the ladies in the room
Standing alone waiting
Fantasizing beautiful women
While lost in the double-cross

Time stained by corruption
And wickedness of the grift
A handful of bills
Evaporate into nothingness
As the pimp disappears
Down a stairway
With the painted ladies
Floating gently above him

A BROTHER'S TYRANNY

She was resigned to her fate
That was borne of the old country
Father taught her the logic
Of the needle and thread
She understood the necessity
Of her older brother's education
That sat heavy on her shoulders
His tyranny without honor
Stole her professional aspirations
The valedictorian owned a paint store
On Oriskany Street in the deep downtown

She sent a monthly payment to her brother
At the dental school
It was an old-fashioned family
Living in an ethnic neighborhood
With arcane customs in food and religion
Love bestowed fortune
Along the carpet toward the future
Her life was permeated in mystery
The son would taste prosperity
Then the daughter

It was prophetic wisdom
Though she endured the bitterness
In her teeth of her brother's ungratefulness
For her sacrifice
As she grew older
She cursed every pain, small or large
A new plague daily
As she aged the bonfires faded
She lived long, dying demented in peace
In her last days she dreamed through delirium
Of her brother holding her tightly in his arms
She saw him clearly standing over her
Urinating on her grave

BLOOD PAINTING

Temple Emmanuel was raped
By two madmen
With four inch horsehair brushes
Drunk ecstatic they painted
A blood red abstract pattern
Over the light beige brick façade

Paint smeared lazily over
The bronze menorah
Protruding from the brick
The desecration with its acid message
Shook the foundation
Of the post World War II
Jewish community

Black and white television portrayed
Emaciated board-like creatures
Tortured in extermination camps
The Jewish community was numb
Shaken with humiliation reliving the horror

A target redrawn on their backs
Looking out through barb-wire
At the stark temple landscape
Knocking the congregation senseless
The floating terror of the Italian ghetto
Inquisitions, burning shtetls
The Crystal Night.

COUSIN LARRY

The angst of sleeping under the pink boulder
Ready to crush the black night at any moment
Could lead all of us to decay
I waited patiently for Larry's e-mail
That was futile since he hates me
Probably believing I'm still in La Paz
Driving shotgun with a band of revolutionaries
Who are tempting to overthrow the Bolivian Government
I know he sees himself as refined

And me a lowly Polish Jew prone to more primitive relationships
With the other sex a bonobo
Touching all the wrong sides of the story while relating
To the most vulnerable young women
He knows I ravaged no child brides
Rumors abound that I traveled with gypsies in Romania
Which is patently false
All I want is a signal, a rogue e-mail
So I know he is alive
He flashes his cold side showing me no love
It hurts like biting your cheek
When appreciating pepper corns
On the most divine filet mignon
I know he's mad for the seething New York City streets
In the village as I'm held in abeyance
Until I hear his beep on my smartphone

GUNSLINGER

Grandpa owned an Army-Navy store
A lion that could easily outflank
His three salesmen
Anxious as gazelles sniffing the air
For predators
A hundred dollars a week
Was their salary
Closing time he'd lock the doors
Cross the railroad tracks
Negotiate the gates
And then drop the proceeds
In the black slot at the bank
Compulsive in routine
He'd pull up his mahogany chair
With red embroidered seat
In front of the TV
Highball in left hand
Cigar in the right
Mirroring the gunslingers
Sitting inside the screen at the bar
Till the westerns killed themselves
Off the air

PIRATES ON MEAD

Nature is spring warblers that rarely stop anymore
Their souls sparkled in springtime
Fluorescent reds orange and yellows
Flash through the nascent leaves on maples and birch
Forty years ago hundreds draped the shrubs
Like an exotic quilt

There are quiet catastrophes that rarely make news
The order of nature shifts before the observant eye
Monsters of energy must be fed
Within boughs of tropical forest
Species once common are scarce
The ruby-throated hummingbird returns each spring
To guzzle like pirates slathered in mead

Six or eight sing squeaky melodies
While dancing in fractal patterns
These emerald beings with dogged determination
Fly along invisible meridians in darkness
Catching celestial guideposts
Surmounting ecological dislocation
Their yearly voyage must not be
Devoid of meaning

STEWARDSHIP

If there are no stewards of our breath
The freshness of air that plant song and dance
Will be lost in a stale fog
Forests will fall to planks covering eroding hills

Children without teachers
Who point the sky and seas alive with mystery
Will be paralyzed to pass knowledge
To steward the unborn

If the dirt is hard, the hands calloused-gloves
The ground ready to give up the harvest
We will still circle the sun during the growing time

If we're crucified with the spines of weeds
That swallow the land
There may be no prophets left
To teach those that might re-claim it

Children cultivating gardens are a brook
That flows to the guardians of the national parks
Lighting up their imaginations by analyzing
A deep breath of fresh air

She said, "Daddy, aren't the silvery robot flowers
Beautiful?" as they sat blinded by the sun
Reflecting off the stainless steel petals

BUTTON BOX

Grandfather immigrated from White Russia to the United States
In the second decade of the twentieth century
Just before the First World War
He was a silent man who often hummed to himself
When he was not in prayer

There was a large steamer
As well as a black Singer sewing machine
In the tailor shop
On special days a jet black box opened to let forth secrets
Of its contents
The most interesting buttons

Buttons that spoke in their own language
Of gemstones, gold, silver, tortoiseshell and pearl
Flashing fountains each with a human form
Standing behind it
They sang of military might and lover's screams
It was difficult to turn from beauty's allure
Their tactile grip held one tight
Like a brother lost or a mother's tears

Each a story inscrutable
As they sat in the black button box
Grandfather may have known their stories
But never spoke of the contents of the box

Buttons worn by the anonymous
Who suffered their loss
Or the prosperous displaying them with pride
To the curious
Mesmerizing the inquisitive
And stroking the forlorn
Buttons humming tales
Lost in mystery
The elder could not divulge

WHITE FOX

White Fox drives through the high mountains
Sloping toward the Pacific
He barters snakes for whiskey and tobacco
With indigenous people living in thatched huts
In the province of Nayarit

Driving is treacherous on the narrow two- lane
Through the Sierra Madre range
With two thousand foot drops reflected in death
Depicted by wooden crosses

Upon his return the back apartment is alive
With canvass bags stuffed with Mexican boa constrictors
Nasty over-sensitive creatures that strike
At the sounds in the room with resonant hissing
Rattlesnakes slither under the beds
Accompanied by large gray iguanas

The serpents are adorned with diamonds and emeralds
Healthy specimens that collectors prefer
Eve is the goddess of serpents
After devouring the apples
No longer is she a naïve child
But a transformed intellect
Encompassing both good and evil intentions

White Fox keeps Eve warm
As the station wagon runs the night
On route to the Texas border

MARTA'S DREAM

Marta wakes, then rolls over in cotton sheets
Deep into dreams
A double below knee amputee
Wheels himself on a plywood platform
Selling small packets of chewing gum
In the Mercado Libertad in Guadalajara
She stares into his sunken eyes
As if her own
The wind fills her sail
She marches into the Sonoran Dessert
Carrying a quart of water

The Harris hawks
Fly from one towering Saguaro to the next
Hungry for flesh
The breeze from the Santa Catalinas
Burns her face like a razor
In the noon sun
Her compass is broken
Lost in the mesquite under the shadows
Of high peaks
Coyotes laugh following her in darkness

A jaguar leaps at her
As she peers at the firmament above
A city in the sky
Floating on points of shimmering light
Sirens wail in the distance
As hunger swallows thought
Vultures sit on her head
Ravens confuse her with questions
Marta screams as she wakes from the nightmare

RODENTS AND LICE

He was a dangerous dreamer of magic words
That fell through his fingers diamonds and sand
He envisioned penny novels that would write themselves
Which were never more than sputtering animations
Across his windows that quickly fell to the night

The kid seemed lost though canaries sang
As they flittered about braiding his hair
He felt gobbled by chimera loping along
Lonely high peaks
A hunter shooting arrows
To bag magic beasts that might change his luck
Chasing fixes in angry neighborhoods
Running from grotesque predatory creatures

He slept more turning stones to pilfer dreams
That might give him seven good years
Waking too many nights to television fuzz
His relativity was skewed
With visions of closing in on the planet of novels
Though he was further than ever
From sitting down with his pen and typewriter

He woke from a nightmare
Where he was smoking a joint in a meth lab
As a professor handed him a degree in nothingness
He lived on iced tea and sugar cubes
Laced with magic potions
While his dreams became infested with rodents and lice
That devoured his novels nascent and pure

HIGH SIERRA

He toddles the first step
Uncertain of destination
Inertia maintains balance
Or there is the fall
Damning the universe
For the misstep
One cycle
Spinning the chain
Gathering momentum
Painting a picture
On the driveway
With a bicycle
A figure eight
Two eyes
Then a mouth
Twisted on moonbeams
Floating over the high sierra

KING KONG 1933

Kong had headlights for eyes, a massive chest and extremities
With a jaded expression of one held too long in captivity
He climbed thirteen hundred feet up the sheer rock face
Of the Empire State Building
Doing battle with confounding technologies
Far from his jungle throne
This behemoth black golem
King of the darkest jungle on the Dark Continent
Running midst a modern creation myth
Of giant apes man and dinosaurs
In the same frame

Anglo blond females in white gowns sacrificed by spooky natives
That shackle hands on a wooden platform behind high gates
Drumming chanting and crashing cymbals
That gains the attention of King Kong
Supreme Being of Skull Island a paradise reversed
Culminating in misogynous love as Ann and the beast cavort
Over a prehistoric landscape

How could a white woman in the south, in 1933,
Wreak such havoc
In a blink the King had gone soft falling hard in love
Saving Ann repeatedly through three King Kong movies
The expedition successfully capturing the poor creature
Shipping him trans-Atlantic to New York City
To his corporate role in chains

The ape in black face bringing big money to a shadowy CEO
He escapes his keepers underestimating
The strength of an angry soul
He tears up Forty-Second Street
Before climbing the towering Empire State Building
Holding Ann in his palm one sweet moment

That brings a flood of tears

As the baddest black man falls as he must
In the pre-World War II South
Where, if there was an alleged contact
Between a black man and white woman
This must always end in tragedy
With the black man hanging from the gibbet
At the end of a tight rope
After emasculation by his white brothers

KILLER

She waited until there was sleep
When we could gravitate toward the other In darkness
Her perfume was irresistible
She responded coming closer under the covers
I slept deeply, feeling tired and weary
In the night I could hear a mariachi band
Sifting in and out of consciousness

There were the love pecks on the cheek
My body tightened as the waterbed sloshed
I rolled out of bed, turned on the light
A chill flowed through me, as if I was dying from flu
She nibbled at my fingers pinching and softly biting
Love bites really, as I regained mindfulness

Then I felt volcanic magma flowing down my leg
My lover tore off her mask revealing the killer within
Exposing herself as an aggressive arachnoid
Twenty minutes elapsed before I discovered her under a boot
Scant red hairs growing from the bulbous abdomen
Five and a half inches of psychopathic spider
Eight sturdy legs extending from her body
Two sword like mandibular fangs

That had envenomed so sweetly
Before grabbing a boot bringing it down harshly
Hearing its hard shell cracking
In the middle of the night
I felt feverish, then fell asleep

SIX CORPSES

First you ask yourself where these people came from
You look around the room and all eyes are drawn to the corner
Where the casks stand
One can almost visualize the contents
The sickly-sweet smell of formaldehyde wafts through the space
Stuck to your nose until much later in the day

For the student there only exists that area of the anatomy
That you will be dissecting
But on this day your attention continues to return to the casks
Holding not wine or bourbon but six stiff corpses
Before each class attendants lift the bodies
By wooden-handled single-pronged steel grappling hooks
From the molasses-colored brine,
Immersed once again in the light of day

These black shrunken withered folks
Caught in the worst sort of spin of the roulette wheel
Face the sharp scalpel daily after sucking in this foul dark solution
That must kill the corpse a second and third time
The poor farmers laborers and brick-layers
Ending their journey in this purgatory
With their flesh stripped away from the bone

One can only wish for a parallel universe that exists
Where they might find redemption
For their souls
Far from the filthy brine where they stand each night
Where instead they think of lovers
They pine for their kisses
Long for a daughter's touch
And glow in joy as they flow through the memory
Of their family and loved ones

SNAKES ON MATTED GRASS

I was young when I took the cruise cruise
Into the vicinity of waterfalls
Where we laid on slabs of sedimentary rock
That held beasties frozen in time
While we broke open the boozy boozy
That tied us to the masts
Swollen with ferocious appetites
Seeped in slime slime
Without inhibitions we danced naked
Under the sun

Smoking exotic leaves
That reversed the flow of rivers
In the brain
Into torrents of thought
Diving off boulders into the swirl swirl
Before we covered our nakedness
With fig leaves and garments
Self-conscious after devouring apples
We played with snakes on matted grass
Until darkness stole the day

COFFEE SHOP EARSHOT

It's an eavesdrop within earshot at the coffee shop
Starbucks Tim Horton dark beans brewed bursting
Over the tongue
A blond beauty reading a review of the latest Coen Brother's
Movie as a brutal weather system beats down on the east coast
Sipping in unison latte and cappuccino
News flash of the President's plan to stop the terrorists
Murder rates climb in Chicago and New York.
Race wars are still critical controversy in the USA
419 scams dot the landscape
They lift their cup high when god and the devil
Enter the banter
All thought flies back to the birth of a thousand
Potentials waking toward the day
As the brain spins to a fine mist like the aroma of
Black coffee wafting through morning traffic

CLOUD FOREST CREATURE

Creatures of cloud forest
React to all before them
From the perspective of wild orchards,
Rivers of ants, flashes like diamonds
In sunlight on butterfly wings
The monkey was as frail
As the stark cardboard box that held him
Purchased as easily as a pup from a kennel
Ten dollars from a Superman
Comic advertisement
A half-century ago

Defensive with resonant hissing and screeching
In prison sentient though dislocated,
Confused about a future with few options
He recalled his past explorations
Over the rain forest canopy

The wild hairy monkey
Looking out through pea-like furtive eyes
Discontented with the turn of events
Pulled like a tooth from the lush forest
Of howls, fragrance, and refuge
Thrown into
A lonely, strange world
With no common language
Tethered to a planet with no atmosphere

RUSSIAN BAR

I'm sitting comfortably at a wooden table
At a Russian bar in Soho
Drinking Stoli with three olives
Midst an ebb and flow of chatter

Rising and falling on the wings of an organ
That sound like Hendrix
Voodoo Child ricocheting back and forth
Through Marshall speakers

I reminisce of friends and lovers
That I imagine are with me
Singing and laughing
As we tip a last round
Before paying my Asian waitress
Thanking her as I walk out the door

The volleys of sound
Following me down Prince Street
As if a demon or a dybbuk
Has jumped down my throat
Enjoying a free ride

BAD FISH

I recall you as that pretty little fillet
Of white fish on ice
I bought you at the Mercado just south
Of Minerva Circle
I cut you up and threw you in
A vegetable broth with sprouts carrots and cabbage
You tasted great in one of my better concoctions
At two AM I awoke in waves of pain
Flashing like heat lightening across my abdomen
Why did you try to kill me?
Did you sense my hubris?
Were you disappointed you were served in soup
And not as the entree
Maybe fish you were a message
I opened pointing to the blackness of my fate
Are you not a devil fish?
Was I detracted by your sweet singing?
Did my enemies fill you with weapons to revenge a vice?
There seemed nothing complicated about you
When I bought you
We're always looking death in the face
But perhaps I didn't recognize her myriad disguises
Fresh fish now spoiled
A good fish gone bad.

AMERICAN BANDSTAND

At a downtown saloon where young pit bulls pulled at leashes
As their ladies beseeched them to stand down
The bedraggled woman followed my eyes through the window
Into the bar
Her skirt was a size large
She wore fake eye lashes with a mangy fox fur around her neck
Complimented by costume jewelry
Emerald brooch and a diamond necklace with matching earrings

Tears dripped down her sunken cheeks
Dick Clark her ex-lover lived in a parallel universe
Intersecting through her own cobwebs of emotion
As she sloshed down beers in a chilly bar
On mean streets that dealt her a three card flush
She looked deep in my eyes
Trying to pull Dick out of a hat
Flopping through sad times
Pickled in the past

Living in a bell-jar hallucinating doo-wop
Riding rivers of set-backs
Dancing cheek to cheek
With social workers and mental health clinics
Waiting for a sign from Dick
Who could pick her up
And fly her away from a downtown
Rotting out from the middle

A baby-Jane caught in a spiral
Of obsession and madness
As the last drops of ale flowed into her glass
The lady palmed a ten dollar bill left on the table
As I disappeared from her night
Imagining Dick and his ex-girlfriend
Each within the other on a 1958 Chris-Craft Capri
As an orange summer sun sets over Hinckley Lake

GOLDEN FROGS

Golden frogs have vanished into the leaf litter
Torn from their tree, lost to eternity
A sudden extinction in primeval forests
Swallowed by invisible warriors
No more forest symphony
The sweet polyphony with piccolo flute
And violin sections in floating harmony
Thrown into the void chewed up by time
No longer mimicking a billion golden suns

Fallen by a crack in their order
Fizzled by radiation losing fight
To the microbes
Intruders have spliced
Their delicate film of existence
The brittle celluloid tears
As its fabric slaps the reel
On the projector
The frog population has been decimated
You can see them in the photographs
In their dark pond

Drinking in the tropical fragrance
Hugging kissing and fornicating
In erotic Bacchanalia
They sing and dance with raucous behavior
Enlivening the forest
Then suddenly like Polaroid prints
Thrown into the fireplace
They twist and turn before being sucked up
The chimney into stardust

ANTIQUITY

Leaves dropped in concentric circles under the oaks
Looking over the valley
An overhang of granite cast shadows
Of indigenous peoples carving stone arrowheads
Protected by stinging red ants
The pyramid rose forty feet
A door led to an inner chamber
With stove and bed

The caretaker offered a sixteenth century bowl
For a hundred pesos
It was life itself chipped and blemished
Through long journey
A vessel born on the breath
Of searing embers
Holding milky molecules that once nourished
Bone and muscle

It had lain in earth absorbing minerals
The elements sealed its strength
It wore its history on its belly
Fixed like a photograph
The multicolored granules stained the bowl
With iron and nickel, toughening its clay

PLAYGROUND MANDALA 1976

I stare at my mandolin,
My fish stare at me as if I were in an aquarium swimming aimlessly
My body feels like it was hit by an Italian earthquake
As I roll out of bed
I am standing over the Pacific mackerel
Last night's meal now caked in its salt
Stinking in the sink along the cracks of my ceramic plate

My blood is going mad; I should've washed the dishes last night
But I felt my eyes were being gobbled up by sleep
Now the fish is swimming upstream, damn-it!
Refusing to be flushed down the drain into the tide of history
This odor cannot be washed off my hands
I will have dreams of Michelangelo being attacked
By a degenerate wino prophet that will drive me to night terrors

The miasma in my sink is haunting me
I sit frozen in my chair staring helplessly at the ski poster on my wall
Thinking about the notes of a guitar in my case singing to themselves
I think I'll take a ride to the country with a friend
Dodging the vicious dogs roving the neighborhood
Watching the water flow down the whistling creeks
Listening to the harmonies of the wind
Spinning on a platform with her in a playground
Everything is moving as I look at the world upside down
From the center of the mandala

BILLIE

Billie felt the pressure,
Each day was like driving
With the valve broken in a tire
The air pushing out of the broken farm
The subsidy from the government
Was barely providing a break even
The dairy farm was small
Run just by Billie and her husband
Her son entertained the idea of buying into the business
But the incentives were never there
Billie recalled the time when she was ice-skating on a pond and broke
Through
Pretty much how she felt all the time now
The milk they sold didn't even pay for the upkeep of the cows

Farming was all Billie knew working was never an issue
Hard work close to the earth was in her bloodline
The figures just weren't adding up
The farm was falling into a sink-hole survival was day to day
They just didn't have the reserves that larger farms had to break even
Billie talked about her youth the simple pleasures
Walking over the hills surrounding the farm
The grasses blowing in a lively wind took her out of the present
The discussion of bankruptcy was the only language
That might open a door

Life was a nightmare
Daile bills came, from a broken milking machine
A car or tractor breaking down, heating a cold house
Or veterinary bills for sick cattle
Billie just had to make her body lighter to stay on top of the quicksand
Her voice was melodious, her smile disarming
Everyone loved her though few could lift her from poverty
Her heart grew weaker she felt failure within an insolvable paradox
It was crushing her
Like the subsidies that barely paid for the gas and heat

Her heart just pumped enough to plant her feet on the ground
Milking for another day
It was telling her that she needed a tombstone
An island that she could call her own
A calm breeze with no guilt or depression
Just peace for eternity
When her heart stopped friends spoke of her courage
Through hard times with no answers
Knowing she was now home

VALUE OF LIFE

Speeding through hairpin turns on the high roads
Cutting through the Sierra Madres
The Renault driven with abandon
Trying to escape the movie
Of flying down a thousand foot canyon face
In the rear view cross and urn
Global positioning the site of death
Socorro says that they don't value life in this country

Cultures of deprivation
Kings and queens worth billions
Bundles of heroin build castles
Politicos control banks of laundered funds
AK47's trump spears,
The infirm jump down rabbit holes
The indigent scattered throughout the planet
Shrouded in darkness

Barbed wire enclosures
Squeeze the spirit off bones,
Bulging eyes seeking to be dealt
In on the winning side
Children eliminating children,
Cutting the roots of civilization

Killing by secret formulas
A quarter of a million deaths
In the space of a dozen dreams of freedom
Commandante thugs rule a terrain
Where life has no value.

CHILDREN IN WHITE ROBES

Brenda waits tables busty blouse tight
She runs past with light exploding in flame
Four kids at home Pyrrhic victory of paychecks
She discorporates into a billion grains of sand
As lecherous men poke eyes on her

She feels strange sensations
The tunneling moles and chipmunks
Share her porous spaces
Rough seas roll over her
Soothing wounds of heart

The waitress would like to take flatterers hostage
She envisions her world an aquarium spawning fish
With sharp teeth
Bridges span from her mind
Allowing her family to walk safely over the sea's sharp scratchings

Bob cuts lumber on a table saw at the mill
Sara house-sits the kids
As Brenda catches tips with her tongue

She daydreams a chain of restaurants
A beast that sprouts arms and legs
Crashes on her beach bringing her great fortune
She throws her elements like an expanding nebula
Over her town
Her head growing large with language,
Geometry and truths

The four horsemen of the apocalypse
Guard her castles
Prisms throw rainbows about her
As she closes the shop

Walking to her car she sees four deer

Grazing in a clearing
They transform into four children
In white robes
Angelic, waiting for tomorrow

TWISTED VIRTUE

Giant mammals facing extinction
Shoulders fifteen feet with tusks hanging
Like two menacing cutlasses from their jaw
Elephants roam with bulls and cows
Cavorting in muddy ponds foraging vegetation
Playfulness representing their world
In their whale-size brain

Self-conscious of missteps
Recalling past migrations
In a mosaic across a mountain range
Killed by death merchants
Who slice tusks from their mouths
With squealing chain saws

Barrages of automatic weapon fire
Leaving the clan in a pile
Under the African sun
Ten thousand grave stones a year
Sacrifices for artistic works of ivory

A curse the bulls wear proudly
Facing genocide from eastern traders
Spinning outlandish tales of black magic
Powdered tusks conferring sexual potency
To men of twisted virtue

THE INVISIBILITY OF OUTRAGE

A young woman returned to her apartment
To grab some books for class
Her boyfriend was there with a friend
After the boyfriend disappeared
The friend pushed her to the ground
And then raped her
In the next month her pregnancy test
Was positive
Her father was a minister
She was humiliated by the event

Never seeking counsel from authorities
Morning after pills were not available
She was self-sufficient quiet and demure
Never wanting to make a scene
Or bring scandal to her family
At first she thought the rapist was kidding
Playing with her until he pushed her face
Into the wooden floor
Pulling off her jeans and penetrating her
As she whimpered the abortion was misery
She tolerated it though her spirit was broken
By the life lost
The consequence remains a vibration that courses
Through a lifetime never forgotten by the victim
For a moment
It ricochets inside a cube within her
Giving dimension to the invisibility of the
Outrage

POETRY READING

I sat waiting for the train that was never on schedule
Niagara Falls to New York City
Looking down the tracks listening for the tenor horn
That shoots through the passengers on the platform like
An invisible wraith
One hour late this time earning the distinction of lost
In sweet time
Living life with zombies too dangerous to invite for dinner
The conductor refuses to punch their ticket
Like a repetitive dream with the same blue eyed boy, blond haired girl
And big dog barking
Waking up a stiff figure restrained in a Broda chair
In his ninth decade moribund yelling expletives
As if giving a poetry reading

VIRTUAL VIRUS RIOT

Stepping into the unknown pressing enter
The search engine explodes into a fairyland
Of bobbing bubble creatures
Born from a cloud painting the screen
With mesmerizing commands
"Essential download"
"Optimize your search"
A warning flashes:
The right click may affect the operation
Of this program
Better surfing on this beach
Staring into a blue horizon
A balloon character reminds one again
That an essential download is required immediately
Soon it's the internal control in the middle brain
That starts flashing warnings with boxed frustration
Oblong foxes jump from eyes
Threatening battle with an imposter robot
Suddenly in full furry the bubbles
Do their crazed dance
Dodging and fainting like a boxer
With a language of beeps and whistles
Those bouncing balls pumped
To be magic men of performance
Beginning to make crunching sounds
Collapsing under the weight of their
Self-destructive impulses
They scheme to infect with the blinking light
As pop-ups begin to paste themselves across the screen

NUTRITIVE ABSENCE

If something went awry
I would wither with you
For we are of the same soil
We thrive on the same vital nutrients
The clear water that kisses my brain
Embraces yours

We are sparrow hawks that push
Against the high air in synchrony
Our gods are of the earth
We are beholden to those
Who have moved humanity
In small steps forward

We play in each other's language
As effortlessly as hummingbirds climb
And swoop invisible half-pipes
When we part
I miss your presence that is mine
You become a hologram in front of me
That is disembodied
I push my hand through you
Without ever touching you
It is then I feel my emptiness
Without you

IRREVERENT CHORUS

The hyena is yapping excited as his troop
Stops at the oasis
Hunger tightens over his gut
His eyes rove slowly focused on shapely
Females sauntering through the crowd

He glances furtively at the women
As saliva collects in his jowl
The spotted coat quivers as he chatters
To the delight of the ladies
Winning a quick blush from his admirers

Lost in laughter and lust
Crusty old males reminisce
Crunching bones from former conquests
As they groom each other
Brashly he licks a female's ear
She reciprocates

Squeezing a last cackle from a petulant female
They all roll in the dust
Yelping as they break camp
The sun high in the blue sky

It is impossible to think in their raucous babbling
The racket shatters concentration
A lion prowls on the border
They are quickly gone
Their snarls faint in the distance

OLD SHOE

These women live in a shoe
One does not see them often
Like snails they stay in their shells
Until they meet necessity
They must put meals on the table

Often you see them
On a sidewalk or shoulder
Of a busy highway
Pushing a grocery cart
That they have borrowed
It is filled with bottles,
Cans and other recyclables

The weather is often inclement
They enliven to an internal imperative
Time has run down
They throw on a ragged green jacket
Facing the elements
As a captain guiding his bark
Through a stormy gale

Each step aggravates
The arthritis in both knees
Her back bent
As she pushes the cart
Onward perhaps another mile
After you've passed her
In your comfortable sedan

You know where she might be headed
There are only so many markets
On this lonely highway
She performs her alchemy
Glass and plastics transformed
Into rations for her family
That live in the old shoe

MONSTERS

Monsters are unrepentant
They serve no captain
Beliefs are secreted to compartments in their interior
Outside controls have minimal effect on them
When an innocent crosses one by error
A bear trap is released upon the careless,
Closing quickly around the body
Causing devastating injury
Victims hover like night moths
That are quickly dispatched in an iron grip

Monster's smiles can be charming
Bringing the unwary into their glue-traps of torture
They are born with a madness pushing for escape
They mimic the tricks of their training
Rarely are they domesticated
Killing and maiming they cleanse themselves
Of the horrors to which they were exposed

Monsters are often invisible,
Fitting in as all the other pegs of society on the great board
They reveal themselves to their prey in infinite manifestations
Monsters are a species ubiquitous on our planet
They are experts in tracking their victim
Through all climates and terrain
One should never underestimate a monster's strengths,
Wile, or will to win and survive
It is nearly unimaginable
To stop a monster's intention
Once set in motion

REFUGEES

The children ask when their father
Will return to this tent civilization
The small ones cry for nurturance
Like dried fruit that long to be kissed
By a sweet mouth
The young take the role of father and mother
Praying for a miracle to reunite them with
Relatives

Deeds and memories are honey and tea
Boredom throws darts of discontent
Rebels march into camp
Firing automatic rifles
As helicopter gunships terrorize
The helpless

Job paints the refugees with doubt
Throwing his bag of woe on them
A father asks when can his family leave
Backs bend backward
Until eyes see only heaven though their
God sleeps

The fabric of reality is soaked in tears
Plans are but promises
Division brings further uncertainty
Dried fruit are scattered in the sand

NIGHTMARES AND GHOSTS

Inferior math teachers provided limited clarity
To calculus and trigonometry problems
He awoke in a sweat
Dreaming of the final examination

A classroom materialized papers rustling
Students delivering finals to a bin
On the wooden desk in the front of the room
While the teacher sifted through their exams

As if struck by lightening
He realized he never attended class
Though it was a requisite for graduation
Numbers running randomly into confusion
The course strangely omitted
Geometry and logic equations
Turning in his brain
Before him a holograph
Three dimensional dreams
Caught in a panic attack

Awakening though still inside them
Breughel's painted landscapes
Of perversions, monstrosities and madness
Cavorting on a thin film of cortex
Awakening to moonlight

A dormant dream leaps off its surface
Into a set of solutions that might satisfy
Requirements for the last semester
He looks down a lonely road equations
Before and aft covering a chalk board

Clarifying mystery while holding his head
Between his hands convincing himself he

Controls his days
Though nightmares and ghosts
Haunt his universe

A Note From the Author

Many poems take form from past memories. They are colored through the prism and nourished by the music of the world. Some are there like whole pictures and words that take up phrase and form. I reach back into my experience, at times allegory or story rings on the page. All my writing is washed with the dream state's diaphanous sphere that saturates my lines with animation and a sense of wonder. Characters in my poems are evil and good. There are bombers, dreamers, environmentalists, gunslingers, and creatures that populate the sensitive ecosystems. I bring emotion and life to elephants, rhinos, birds and the human experience. I create tension, imagining individuals in dangerous situations that recall my life experiences. Writing is a pleasure with satisfaction of a runner's high. Likewise droughts are frustrating. I've written seriously for the last four years. In addition to poetry I've written parables and fables. It is a great pleasure for me to watch someone read my work or listen to my poetry.

Acknowledgements

I would like to thank these individuals for their role in bringing CROWS NEST to fruition. I want to sincerely thank Mark Pogodzinski for his silent good judgment in bringing this project forward. I want to thank Fred Whitehead for solidifying Mark as my publisher. My mother for her interest and support of my writing. Karen for her fine editorial reflexes early on in this project. My wife Wendy for her assistance in pulling diverse aspects of the poetry book together. My brother, Noah for his poetic sculptural constructs and fertile mind.

www.ingramcontent.com/pod-product-compliance
Lightning Source LLC
Chambersburg PA
CBHW032050040426
42449CB00007B/1053